Chinese:

Learn Chinese In 21 DAYS!

A Practical Guide To Make Chinese Look Easy! EVEN For Beginners

Table Of Contents

Introduction

This book contains 21 highly-informative chapters on the fundamentals of Mandarin Chinese, the most widely spoken language in the world. It is written to address the needs of travellers, entrepreneurs, and students who want to have a good grasp of the language in no time at all. This book is designed for beginners and intermediate learners of Chinese who prefer to learn at their own pace and convenience. It aims to provide self-learners an excellent foundation of the language by imparting essential grammar features, pronunciation, vocabulary, and key phrases in everyday conversations.

The book starts with a few chapters on the basics of the Chinese language — pronunciation, numbers, telling time, months, days, and seasons, telling the year and date, colors, and common greetings. The succeeding chapters cover grammar topics such as parts of speech, word order, forming questions, making comparisons, and other unique features of Mandarin.

Each grammar lesson is presented in a straightforward manner and features relevant examples and charts, which were carefully selected and created to enhance the learner's comprehension and appreciation of the language, as well as to shorten learning time considerably. Finally, to fast-track your learning path, the book provides vocabulary listings as well as common phrases for different occasions — introducing yourself, talking about your family, asking for directions, eating out, shopping, booking a hotel, and getting around.

Let's begin the journey.

Chapter 1: The Basics of Mandarin Chinese

One of the most important steps in learning the Chinese language is getting acquainted with its pronunciation. For beginners in the study of the Chinese language, the best places to start are Pinyin and the four tones of Mandarin. In this chapter, you will learn how to pronounce Mandarin words by familiarizing yourself with Pinyin and the four tones. In the succeeding sections, you will be acquainted with Chinese cardinal and ordinal numbers, colors, common greetings, and useful everyday phrases.

Pronunciation

Hanyu Pinyin, or simply Pinyin, is the official phonetic system used to convert Mandarin Chinese sounds into the Latin alphabet. It is the most common Romanized version of the Chinese language. Pinyin was invented in the 1950s and has since been used as a standard for teaching Chinese in Mainland China, as well as in other parts of the world.

Mandarin has sounds that have no equivalent in English and learning Pinyin is important if you want to know how to pronounce Mandarin properly. With regular practice and repetition, you can master the Mandarin sound in no time at all.

One Pinyin can be considered as one syllable. Every Pinyin consists of three parts: an initial, a final, and a tone. For example, in the word "wǒ", "w" is the initial, "o" is the final, and the mark above the "o"is the tone. You can think of initials as the equivalent of consonants in English and the finals as the vowels.

Here are the 21 initials (consonants) in Chinese:

b p m f g k h j d t n l s zh ch sh r q
x z c

The finals (vowels) are listed here:

a ai ao an ang

o ou ong

e er ei en eng

i ia iao ie iu iam in iang ing iong

u ua uo uai ui uan un uang ueng

ü üe üan ün

Following is the Mandarin Chinese pronunciation based on Pinyin. You must familiarize yourself with the Mandarin pronunciation before proceeding to other lessons.

Pinyin	Approximate Sound	Example
b	like the 'b' in 'bay' but softened to closely approach the 'p' sound	bā
p	like the 'p' in 'pay' but with more aspiration	pā

m	like the 'm' in 'morning'	mà
f	same as the 'f' in 'fan'	fá
d	like the 'd' in 'day' but softened to approach the sound of 't'	dā
t	like the 't' in 'tough' but with more aspiration	tă
n	like the 'n' in 'none'	té
l	like the 'l' in 'love'	lē
g	like the 'g' in 'grill but softened to approach the sound of 'k'	gān
k	like the 'k' in 'kit' or 'keen' but with more aspiration	kāi
h	like the 'h' in 'hay' but with a heavier sound	hē
j	close to the sound of 'j' in 'jeep' — the tongue touches the lower teeth	jí
q	like the 'ch' in 'chair' — the tip of the tounge touches the lower teeth	qí
x	close to the sound of 'sh' in 'sheep' — the tip of the tongue touches the lower teeth	xīn
zh	like the 'j' in 'jump' with the tongue curled	zhā

	upwards	
ch	like the 'ch' in 'cheap' with the tongue curled upwards	chā
sh	similar to the 'sh' in 'marsh' with the tongue curled upwards	shá
r	close to the 'r' in 'rough' with the tongue curled upwards	rāo
z	like the ending 'dz' sound in 'kids'	zé
c	like the 'ts' in 'cats'	cā
s	like the 's' in 'sun'	sē
i	like the 'ee' in 'see' (with an exception — see below)	xī
i	after r, sh, zh, ch — like the 'ir' in 'shirt' but the 'r' has a lighter sound	chī
i	after z, c, s, — like the 'I' in 'sit'	zī
u	like the 'oo' in 'broom'	bū
iu/yu	similar to the 'yo' in 'yoyo'	yǒu
a	like the 'a' in 'father'	pà
o	like the 'o' in 'more'	bō

e	similar to the 'uh' in 'duh'	mē
er	like the 'e' in 'teacher'	ér
ie/ye	like the 'ye' in 'yellow'	léi
ai	like the 'eye'	pài
ei	like the 'ay' in 'pay' or the 'ei' in 'weigh'	tēi
ia/ya	combines 'ee' + 'a' — you must pronounce this very quickly to blend the two vowels	lià
ao	similar to the 'ow' in 'cow' but longer	báo
ou	like the 'ou' in 'dough'	mōu
an	like the 'an' in the 'fan'	kàn
en	like the 'en' in the 'taken'	děn
un	combines 'oo' + 'en' and sound like 'uen'	gūn
in	like 'een' in 'teen'	nín
ua/wa	combines 'oo' + 'a'	guā
ui/wei	combines 'oo' + 'ay'	dūi
uo/wo	combines 'oo' + 'o'	duō
ang	combines the sound of 'a' in 'father' and the 'ng' in 'sing'	lāng

eng	combines the sound of 'uh' in 'duh' and the 'ng' in 'sing'	zēng
ong	combines the sound of 'o' in 'more' and the 'ng' in 'sing'	gōng
ing	combines the sound of 'ee' + 'ng'	līng
iao/yao	combines the sound of 'ee' + 'ow' in 'cow'	diáo
ian/yan	combines the sound of 'ee' + 'an'	dián
iong/yong	combines the sound of 'ee' + 'ong'	giōng
iang/yang	combines the sound of 'ee' + 'ang'	niáng
uai/wai	combines the sound of 'oo' + 'eye'	kuái
uan/wan	combines the sound of 'oo' + 'an'	guān
uang/wang	combines the sound of 'oo' + 'ang'	guāng
ueng/weng	combines the sound of 'oo' + 'eng'	
ü	say 'cheeeeese' while rounding out your lips, no similar English sound	nü
üe/yue	combines ü + 'e' in 'yet'	nüe

üan/yuan	combines ü + 'an' in 'fan'	jüan
ün/yun	combines ü + 'en' in 'taken'	

Chapter 2: The Four Tones in Mandarin

Mandarin is a tonal language which means that a syllable can have different meanings depending on the tone used by the speaker. Mandarin has four tones plus a neutral tone. The tones used in Mandarin give the language a distinctive quality and must be learned closely to avoid miscommunication.

The First Tone

The first tone is high and even. When using this tone, it is important to keep your voice flat in an almost monotone way. This tone is indicated by a horizontal line above the letter or by writing number '1' at the end of the syllable.

Example:

Pinyin	Chinese	Meaning
mā	妈	mother

The Second Tone

The second tone rises moderately with your voice starting at a low pitch and rising to a middle pitch — very similar to how you would ask a question in English. It is indicated by a rising diagonal line on top of the letter or in some cases, by the number '2' at the end of the syllable.

Example:

Pinyin	Chinese	Meaning
má	麻	hemp

The Third Tone

The third tone is a dipping tone where your voice begins at middle pitch, falls to a low pitch, then rises to a high pitch. It is indicated by a "dipping" or curved line above the letter or in some cases, by the number '3' at the end of the syllable.

Example:

Pinyin	Chinese	Meaning
mǎ	马	horse

The Fourth Tone

The fourth tone starts at a high pitch and drops rapidly to a low pitch. It is the tone you would normally use in English when issuing an angry command. The tone is indicated by a dropping diagonal line on top of the letter or in some instances, by writing number '4' at the end of the syllable.

Example:

Pinyin	Chinese	Meaning
mà	骂	to scold

Chapter 3: Counting and Numbers

Counting in Mandarin

Learning to count in Chinese is much easier than you think. In fact, just by using 13 syllables, you can already count up to 9,999.

To count from 1 to 99, you need to learn the numbers 1 to 10. From 11 to 19, just add "shí" (ten) before the units digit (1-9). Hence, 11 is expressed as "shí yī" (10-1) and 15 is expressed as shí wǔ (10-5). To count from 20 onwards, the tens are expressed as "èr shí" (2-10) for 20, sān shí (3-10) for 30, and jiǔ shí (9-10) for 90.

To express 31, you'll say "sān shí yī" (3-10-1) and to express 95, you'll say "jiǔ shí wǔ" (9-10-5).

When used as is, the number 100 is expressed as "yī bǎi" but if you add a unit digit from 1 to 9, you will have to state the zero. For instance, 101 is "yì bǎi líng yī" (100-0-1) and 102 is "yì bǎi líng èr" (100-0-2). To express 110, you just say "yì bǎi yī shí" (100-10).

Did you notice how the "yī"(first tone) changed to "yì" (fourth tone) when you use 100 before other numbers? On its own, 100 takes the first tone but when it comes before syllables using the first, second, or third tone, the number shifts to the fourth tone.

While you may find it easy to count from 1 to 9,999, numbers starting from 10,000 can pose challenges. In Chinese, large numbers from 10,000 to 99,999,999 are expressed based on the number of ten thousands they have. The first 10,000 digit is represented by wàn (万). Hence, to express the equivalent of 10,000 in Chinese, you'll say "yī wàn" or "1 ten thousand". To express 50,000, you'll say "wǔ wàn" or "5 ten thousand". One million is expressed as "yī bǎi wàn" or "100 ten thousand". When the number reaches 100,000,000 million, you'll use another classifier, "yì" (亿) which represents one hundred million. Hence, to express 100,000,000, you'll say "yī yì" or "1 one hundred million".

There are two ways of writing numbers in Mandarin. One is the simple form which is used in everyday counting needs. The other is the complex form which is used in financial transactions, bank notes, checks, and other bank documents.

Cardinal Numbers

Here are the cardinal numbers in Mandarin and their corresponding simple and complex forms:

Number	Simple Numerals	Complex Numerals	Pinyin
0	〇	零	líng
1	一	壹	yī
2	二	貳	èr / liǎng
3	三	叁	sān
4	四	肆	sì
5	五	伍	wǔ
6	六	陸	lìu
7	七	柒	qī
8	八	捌	bā
9	九	玖	jiǔ
10	十	拾	shí
11	十一	拾壹	shí yī
12	十二	拾貳	shí èr
13	十三	拾叁	shí sān
14	十四	拾肆	shí sì

15	十五	拾伍	shí wǔ
16	十六	拾陸	shí lìu
17	十七	拾柒	shí qī
18	十八	拾捌	shí bā
19	十九	拾玖	shí jiǔ
20	二十	貳拾 [廿]	èr shí [ni àn]
21	二十一	貳拾壹	èr shí yī
22	二十二	貳拾貳	èr shí èr
23	二十三	貳拾叁	èr shí sān
24	二十四	貳拾肆	èr shí sì
25	二十五	貳拾伍	èr shí wǔ
26	二十六	貳拾陸	èr shí lìu
27	二十七	貳拾柒	èr shí qī
28	二十八	貳拾捌	èr shí bā
29	二十九	貳拾玖	èr shí jiǔ
30	三十	叁拾 [卅]	sān shí [sà]
31	三十一	叁拾壹	sān shí yī

32	三十二	叁拾贰	sān shí èr
33	三十三	叁拾叁	sān shí sān
34	三十四	叁拾肆	sān shí sì
35	三十五	叁拾伍	sān shí wǔ
36	三十六	叁拾陆	sān shí lìu
37	三十七	叁拾柒	sān shí qī
38	三十八	叁拾捌	sān shí bā
39	三十九	叁拾玖	sān shí jiǔ
40	四十	肆拾 [卌]	sì shí [xì]
50	五十	伍拾	wǔ shí
60	六十	陆拾	lìu shí
70	七十	柒拾	qī shí
80	八十	捌拾	bā shí
90	九十	玖拾	jiǔ shí
100	一百	壹佰	yī bǎi
101	一百〇一	壹佰零壹	yì bǎi

			líng yī
102	一百〇零二	壹佰零貳	yì bǎi líng èr
125	一百二十五	壹佰貳拾伍	yì bǎi èr shí wǔ
1,000	一千	壹仟	yī qiān
1,001	一千〇一	壹仟零壹	yì qiān líng yī
10,000	一万	壹萬	yī wàn
1 million	一百万	壹佰萬	yī bǎi wàn
100 million	一亿	壹億	yī yì
1 billion	十亿	拾億	shí yì
1 trillion	一兆	壹兆	yī zhào

Chapter 4: Two ways to say number "two"

Chinese uses two words to express the number "two", èr 二 and liǎng 两.

Èr

- Èr is used when counting in general, when referring to the number "two" itself, in phone numbers and similar figures, and when there are no measure words.

Example:

Counting one to five: -> yī, èr, sān, sì, wǔ – one, two, three, four, five

- The èr form is also used for bigger numbers ending in two such as 22, 52, 122, 1002, etc. whether or not a measure word is used.

Examples:

èr shí èr běn shū -> twenty-two books

yì bǎi líng èr ge rén -> one hundred two people

yì qiān líng èr kuài qián -> one thousand two dollars

- The èr form is also used with dì (第) to express the ordinal number "second"

dì èr -> 第二 -> the second

èr lóu -> 二楼 -> the second floor

Liǎng   两

- Liǎng is used with measure words.

Mandarin requires measure words when quantifying nouns or objects. The most common form is ge 個/个 which is used for people but may also be used for other nouns. Běn 本 is another measure word which is used for books. You use liǎng to express two of something.

The format for expressing the quantity of a specific noun is "number + measure word + object".

Examples:

two people -> liǎng ge rén

two books -> liǎng běn shū

two weeks -> liǎng gè xīng qī ->两个星期

two months -> liǎng gè yuè ->两个月

- Some numbers take the liǎng form:

two hundred -> liǎng bǎi

two thousand -> liǎng bǎi

twenty thousand -> liǎng wàn

- Liǎng is used for expressing time at two o'clock:

2 o'clock -> liǎng diǎn -> 两点

Take note that some numbers also function as measure words:

bǎi -> hundred

qiān -> thousand

wàn -> ten thousand

You will find the following list of Chinese measure words handy:

Nouns	Pinyin	Simplified	Traditional
books	běn	本	本
bottles	píng	瓶	瓶
buildings	dòng	栋	棟
clothing	jiàn or tào	件 or 套	件 or 套
doors and windows	shàn	扇	扇
flat objects (tables, paper)	zhāng	张	張
heavy objects (appliances, machines)	tái	台	台
letters and mails	fēng	封	封
long round objects (pencils, pens)	zhī	支	支
people	gè or wèi	个 or 位	個 or 位
periodicals	qī	期	期
portions	fèn	份	份
rooms	jiān	间	間

trees	kē	棵	棵
vehicles	liàng	辆	輛
written sentences	jù	句	句

Ordinal Numbers

Chinese ordinal numbers are quite easy to form if you know the cardinal numbers. You will just have to add "dì (第)" before the number.

Mandarin ordinal numbers:

1st	dì yī	第一
2nd	dì èr	第二
3rd	dì sān	第三
4th	fourth	第四
5th	dì wǔ	第 五
6th	dì liù	第六
7th	dì qī	第七
8th	dì bā	第八
9th	dì jiǔ	第九

10th	dì shí	第十
15th	dì shí wǔ	第十五
21st	dì èr shí yī	第二十一
66th	dì liù shí liù	第六十六
145th	dì yī bǎi sì shí wǔ	第一百四十五

Here are sentences using cardinal numbers:

Nǐ shì dì yī. 你是第一。-> You are the first.

Tā shì dì sì. -> 她是第四。-> She was fourth.

Days, Months, and Seasons

Days of the Week

Days of the week in Mandarin are pretty straightforward. First of all, you have to know these terms which both mean "week":

zhōu -> 周

xīng qī-> 星期

Now, to express the day, just say "xīng qī + 1 to 6" for Mondays to Saturdays with Monday as day 1, Tuesday as day 2, and so on. Sunday is a special day that you have to memorize.

Monday	xīng qī yī	星期一
Tuesday	xīng qī èr	星期二
Wednesday	xīng qī sān	星期三
Thursday	xīng qī sì	星期四
Friday	xīng qī wǔ	星期五
Saturday	xīng qī liù	星期六
Sunday	xīng qī tiān	星期天

Months of the Year

Months of the year in Mandarin are just as easy to remember. You only need to learn the term for month and the numbers 1 to 12:

Month: -> yuè -> 月

January	yī yuè	一月
February	èr yuè	二月
March	sān yuè	三月
April	sì yuè	四月
May	wǔ yuè	五月
June	liù yuè	六月

July	qī yuè	七月
August	bā yuè	八月
September	jiǔ yuè	九月
October	shí yuè	十月
November	shí yī yuè	十一月
December	shí èr yuè	十二月

UsefulExpressions:

Pinyin	Chinese	English
měi	每	every
měitiān	每天	every day
qián tiān	前天	2 days ago
zuó tiān	昨天	yesterday
jīn tiān	今天	today
míng tiān	明天	tomorrow
hòutiān	后天	the day after tomorrow
qiǎntiān	前天	the day before yesterday
hòu tiān	后天	in two days
liǎng gè xīng qī qián	两个星期前	two weeks ago

shàng gè xīng qī	上个星期	last week
zhè ge xīng qī	这个星期	this week
xià gè xīng qī	下个星期	next week
liǎng gè xīng qī hòu	两个星期后	2 weeks from now
liǎng gè yuè qián	两个月前	two months ago
shàng gè yuè	上个月	last month
zhè ge yuè	这个月	this month
xià gè yuè	下个月	next month
liǎng gè yuè hòu	两个月后	two months from now
qián nián	前年	two years ago
qù nián	去年	last year
jīn nián	今年	this year
míng nián	明年	next year
hòu nián	后年	two years from now
qù nián	去年	last year
měi nián	每年	every year
měi yī nián	每一年	each year

hòu nián	后年	they year after next
qián nián	前年	the year before last

Seasons (jìjié 季节)

dōngtiān	冬天	Winter
chūntiān	春天	Spring
xiàtiān	夏天	Summer
qiūtiān	秋天	Autumn

Epressing Duration:

To express duration in Mandarin, you'll have to state the number and the unit. Here are common expressions in duration:

_____ fēnzhōng 分钟 -> _____ minute(s)

_____ xiǎoshí 小时 -> _____ hour(s)

_____ tiān 天 -> _____ day(s)

_____ xīngqī 星期 -> _____ week(s)

_____ yùe 月 -> _____ month(s)

_____ nián 年 -> _____ year(s)

Chapter 5: Telling the Date

To express the date, you'll name the month first and then the day followed by either rì (日) or hào (号). Hào (号) is more often used in spoken Mandarin while rì (日) is more frequently used in written documents.

To tell the date in the long format, you'll start from the biggest to the smallest block of time. For example, here is how you will say, "Today is February 28, 2016, Sunday" in Mandarin:

Jīntiān shì èr ling yī liù nián èr yuè èr shí bā hào, xīng qī tiān

Colors in Mandarin

Color	Pinyin	Chinese
Red	hóng sè	紅色
Blue	lán sè	藍色
White	bái sè	白色
Yellow	huáng sè	黃色
Orange	jú sè or chéng sè	橘色 or 橙色
Green	lǜ sè	綠色
Brown	kāfēi sè	咖啡色
White	bái sè	白色

Black	hēi sè	黑色
Grey	huī sè	灰色
Purple	zǐ sè	紫色

Common Greetings and Useful Expressions

nin hǎo	您好	Hello! (polite form)
wéi (on the phone)	喂	Hello!
nǐ hǎo ma?	你好嗎?	How are you?
nín hǎo ma?	您好嗎?	How are you? (polite form)
nǐ dzěmuhyàng?	你怎麼樣?	What's up?
wǒ hěn hǎo. xiè xiè nín.	我很好 谢谢您 。	I'm fine. Thank you.
nǐ guìxìng dàmíng?	你貴姓大名？	What's your name?
nǐ jiào shénme míngzì?	你叫什麼名字？	What's your name?
wǒ xìng ____	我姓 —	My name is _____

wǒ jiào ____	我叫 ──	My name is _____
xìnghuì!	幸會	Nice to meet you!
wǒ ài nǐ	我愛你	I love you.
wǒ xiǎngniàn nǐ	我想念你	I miss you.
dzǎo-anh	早安	Good morning.
dzǎo	早	Good morning.
zǎo chén hǎo.	早晨好。	Good morning.
ǔ-anh	午安	Good afternoon (seldom used)
xìa-ǔ hǎo	下午好	Good afternoon (seldom used)
wǎn-anh	晚安	Good night.
wǎn shang hǎo	晚上好	Good evening.
dzàijien	再見	See you again.
míngtien jien	明天見	See you tomorrow.
huítów jien	回頭見	See you soon.
zhù nǐ háoyùn	祝你好運	Good luck!
kuài diǎn hào la	快點好	Get well soon.

	啦	
shēngrì kuàilè	生日快樂	Happy birthday.
gōngxǐ fācái	恭喜發財	Chinese New Year greetings
zhèng què.	正确	Yes.
cuò wù.	错误。	No.
qǐng.	请	Please.
xièxiè nín.	谢谢您。	Thank you.
bú kè qì.	不客气。	You're welcome.
dùi bù qǐ.	对不起。	I am sorry.
láo jià.	劳驾。	Excuse me.
méiguānxi	没关系	It's okay.
qǐng rùxí	請入席	Please take a seat.
wǒ bú míng bái.	我不明白	I don't understand.
wǒ bù zhīdào	我不知道	I don't know.
nín shūo shén me?	您说什么?	What did you say?

wǒ míngbai	我明白	I understand.
zhège duōshǎo qián?	這個多少錢？	How much is this?
cèsuǒ zài nǎli?	廁所在哪裡？	Where's the toilet?
xǐ shǒujiān zài nǎli?	洗手间在哪里？	Where's the bathroom?
jiùmìng ā!	救命啊!	Help!
jiào jǐngchá	叫警察!	Call the police!
búyào dǎrǎo wǒ!	不要打扰我	Leave me alone!
tíngxià!	停下!	Stop!
tíng chē	停車!	Stop! (to someone in vehicle)
zhànzhù	站住!	Stop! (to someone on foot)
wǒ mílù le	我迷路了。	I'm lost.
wǒ shēngbìng	我生病了。	I'm sick.
wǒ xūyào yīshēng	我需要医生。	I need a doctor.

Chapter 6: Telling Time

Being able to tell time is an important aspect of learning a language. You use time to talk about your schedule and make travel arrangements, among others. In this chapter, you will learn how to ask for and tell time in Mandarin.

To ask for time in Chinese, you can use this phrase:

Xiànzài jī diǎn le? -> 現在幾點了? -> What time is it?

Telling time in Mandarin is a bit different from telling time in English, but if you know how to count in Mandarin, you will just use some new words to tell the specific time.

To tell the general and specific time, you will need the following terms:

diǎn	点	o'clock
kè	刻	a quarter of
bàn	半	half
chà	差	be short of/to
fēn zhōng	分鐘	minute

fēn	分	minute
zǎo shang	早上	morning
shàng wǔ	上午	morning
zhōng wǔ	中午	noon
xià wǔ	下午	afternoon
wǎn shang	晚上	evening
yè lǐ	夜裡	night
bàn yè	半夜	midnight
xiànzài	现在	now
yǐhòu	以后	later
shāohòu	稍后	later
yǐqián	以前	before

Telling time in Chinese is a lot like reading the time in a digital clock. You'll read the hours the way you would a regular number in Mandarin, substitute 'diǎn' for the colon or double dots, then state the minutes number and add the word 'fēn' for minutes.

For instance, when the time is at 9:05, you can say 'jiǔ diǎn wǔ fēn' which literally means nine o'clock five minutes.

- When the minute is on the half hour, you'll use the word 'bàn' after 'diǎn' to indicate that it's half hour or 30 minutes past the hour.

Example:

When the time is at 10:30, you can say 'shí diǎn bàn'. Literally, this means 10 o'clock half.

Similarly, when the time is at 9:30, you'll say 'jiǔ diǎn bàn'.

- When the time is fifteen minutes or one quarter past an hour, you can use the expression 'yī kè', literally one quarter, after diǎn. You may also choose to just state the actual minutes and add fēn after the number.

Example:

To express that it is 6:15, you can say 'liù diǎn yī kè' 六点一刻. Literally, it's 6 o'clock one quarter.

Alternatively, you can say fifteen minutes after the hour. For example, to express time at 12:15, you can say: 'shí èr diǎn shí wǔ fēn'. You can read this as twelve o'clock fifteen minutes.

- When the time is a few minutes short of the approaching hour, you can use the word 'chà' to indicate the number of minutes before the coming hour.

Example:

When the time is at 10:55, you can say: 'chà wǔ fēn shí yī diǎn' 差五分十一点 – to express that it is five minutes to 11 o'clock.

- To indicate the part of day, you'll have to use appropriate time expressions before the time. Take note of this convention in Chinese time and date expressions. Time units are arranged from the biggest to the smallest time block. Hence, phrases pertaining to the general time of day are placed in front of the time expression.

For instance, to say 'It is 9 in the morning', you'll say 'zǎoshàng jiǔ diǎn zhōng.'

Other Examples:

8:00 AM -> zǎo shang bā diǎn -> 早上八點

9:05 PM -> wǎn shang jiǔ diǎn wǔ fēn -> 晚上九點五分

9:30 -> jiǔ diǎn bàn -> 九点半

2:00 PM -> xià wǔ liǎng diǎn ->　下午兩點

9:05 PM -> wǎn shang jiǔ diǎn wǔ fēn ->　晚上九點五分

1:30 PM -> xiàwǔ yīdiǎn bàn ->　下午一点半

Useful time phrases:

xiàwǔ èr diǎn qián ->　下午二点前 -> before 2 PM

zhōngwǔ zhì wǔyè　->　中午至午夜 -> noon to midnight

wǔyè dào liming ->　午夜到黎明 -> midnight to dawn

wǎn shàng qī diǎn zhì wǔyè　晚上 7 点至午夜 -> 7 PM to midnight

Chapter 7: Mandarin Grammar

Nouns

Chinese nouns have the following characteristics:

- They have no separate form for the plural. Plurality is indicated by numerals or modifiers.

- Chinese nouns are almost always modified by a measure word.

- They may function as a subject, a complement, or an object.

- Chinese nouns may sometimes be used as adverbial but not as a result.

- Nouns are usually not reduplicated.

- They cannot be modified or negated by bù 不.

- Chinese nouns have no possessive case. Possession is indicated by the particle (de) 的.

Using de 的 to Show Possession

In general, the particle de 的 is placed after the noun to show possession in Chinese. The structure is:

Subject (Noun/Pronoun) + 的 (de) + Noun 2

The subject may refer to any type of noun or a pronoun while Noun 2 is the subject's possession.

Examples:

father's car -> bàba de chē -> 爸爸 的 车

my teacher -> wǒ de lǎoshī -> 我 的 老师

your money -> nǐ de qián -> 你的 钱

our food -> wǒmen de cài -> 我们的 菜

the company's boss -> gōngsī de lǎobǎn -> 公司 的 老板

my friend -> wǒ de péngyou -> 我 的朋友

your cellphone -> nǐ de shǒujī -> 你 的 手机

The particle de 的, however may be omitted in the following cases:

- When it involves a close personal relationship
- When it involves an organizational or institutional relationship

Examples:

My mom is very beautiful. -> **Wǒ māmā** hěn piàoliang. -> 我妈妈很 漂亮

This is **my girlfriend**. -> Zhè shì **wǒ nǚpéngyou**. -> 这 是 我 女朋友

My house is very big -> **Wǒ jiā** hěn dà. -> 我 家 很 大

My son is very tall. -> Wǒ érzi hěn gāo. -> 我儿子很 高

Their company is in Shanghai. -> Tāmen gōngsī zài shànghǎi . 他们 公司 在上海

Modifying nouns with an adjective and de 的

In English, you can easily modify nouns by placing adjectives before them.

Examples: beautiful girl, big house, new car, thick books, lovely flowers

In Chinese, you will have to use the particle de 的 to attach an adjective to a noun. The structure is:

Adjective + de 的 + Noun

Examples:

beautiful girl -> piàoliang de nǚháir -> 漂亮 的 女孩儿

a cute baby -> kě'ài de bǎobǎo -> 可爱 的 宝宝

spicy food -> là de cài -> 辣 的 菜

In some instances, you can omit the noun from the pattern and simply use the adjective and de 的 to mean "the yellow one" or "the tall one". In such cases, "de" functions as "one" in the sentence. When using this, pattern, however, you have to make sure that the other person knows which "one" you're talking about. This pattern may only be used if the subject has been identified previously in the conversation or when responding to a question.

For example:

A: What food do you like to eat? -> Nǐ xǐhuān chī shénme shíwù 你喜欢吃什么食物

B: Sweet ones. -> Tián de. 甜 的 。

Modifying nouns with phrase and de 的

Besides attaching adjectives to modify a noun, the particle de 的 can likewise be used to associate phrases to nouns. This pattern is the equivalent of "who", "that", or "which" in English. For instance, in English you might say "the man who saw tomorrow" or "the car that he bought last year".

The pattern for this usage is:

Phrase + de 的 + Noun where the phrase is a verb+(object)

Examples:

the books that **she wrote -> tā xiě** de shū -> 她 写 的 书

the pictures that **he drew -> tā huà** de huà -> 他 画 的画

the women who wear Prada -> **chuān Prada** de nǚrén -> 穿-> **Prada** 的 女人

Nouns of Locality

In Chinese, the nouns of locality are used to indicate location. These words are not prepositions although they are translated as such in English. Here are examples:

One-Character	Two-Character	English
shàng	shàngmiàn /	top, above

上	shàngbiān 上面、上边	
xià 下	下面、下边	bottom, under
lǐ 里	里面、里边	inside
wài 外	外面、外边	outside
biān 边	pángbiān 旁边	side, beside
qián 前	前面、前边	front
hòu 后	后面、后边	back, behind
zuǒ 左	左边	left
yòu 右	右边	right

Chapter 8: Pronouns 代词 (dàicí)

Subject and Object Pronouns:

Mandarin Chinese uses three basic pronouns which have the same form whether they're used as subject or object in a sentence. Hence, when constructing sentences, you have to be careful about how the words are arranged.

I, me -> wǒ

you -> nǐ

he, him / she, her / it -> tā

There is only one third person pronoun in Pinyin and it stands for 'he', 'she', and 'it': tā. Be aware, however, that there are distinct Chinese characters for the third person:

he -> 他

she -> 她

it -> 它

Plural Form of Pronouns

To form the plural, you will just have to add "men" at the end of the singular pronoun form. Hence:

we, us -> wǒ men

you -> nǐ men

they, them -> tā men

The pronoun "you" has a polite form in Mandarin which you will normally use when addressing someone who is older or a superior:

You -> nǐn

Subject and Object Pronouns Chart

Singular			Plural		
I, me	wǒ	我	we, us	wǒ men	我们
you	nǐ	你	you (plural)	nǐmen	你们
you (polite)	nín	您			

he, him	tā	他	they,them	tā men	他们
she, her	tā	她	they, them	tā men	她们
it	tā	它	they,them	tā men	它们

Usage of Pronouns:

Wǒ - 我

Wǒ shì kuàijì.

我是会计。

I am an accountant.

Wǒ xǐhuān bīngqílín.

我喜欢冰淇淋。

I like ice cream.

I don't have a car.

Wǒ méi yǒu chē.

我没有车。

Nǐ - 你

Nǐ shì kuàijì ma?

你是会计吗?

Are you an accountant?

Nǐ xǐhuan bīngqílín ma?

你喜欢冰淇淋吗?

Do you like ice cream?

Tā - 他 她 它

Tā shì yīshēng.

他是医生。

He is a doctor.

Tā xǐhuan kāfēi.

她喜欢咖啡。

She likes coffee.

Tā méi yǒu chē.

他没有车。

He doesn't have a car.

Wǒmen - 我們

Wǒmen shì lǜshī.

我们是律师。

We are lawyers.

Wǒmen xǐhuan bīngqílín.

我们喜欢冰淇淋。

We like ice cream.

Tāmen - 他們

Tāmen shì xuéshēng.

他们是学生。

They are students.

Tāmen xǐhuan kāfēi.

他们喜欢咖啡。

They like coffee.

Tāmen méi yǒu jiǎotàchē.

他们没有脚踏车。

They don't have a bicycle.

Possessive Pronouns

To form the possessive pronoun in Mandarin, just add "de" after the basic pronoun.

Singular			Plural		
my, mine	wǒ de	我的	our, ours	wǒmen de	我们的
your,	nǐ	你	your, yours	nǐmen	你们

yours	de	的		de	的
your, yours (polite form)	nín de	您 的	your, yours (polite form)	nínmen de	您 们 的
his	tā de	他 的	their,theirs	tāmen de	他 们 的
her, hers	tā de	她 的	their, theirs	tāmen de	她 们 的
its	tā de	它 的	their,theirs	tāmen de	它 们 的

Reflexive Pronouns

Chinese uses a reflexive pronoun, zìjǐ -自己, when the subject and object refer to the same person. For example:

He likes himself. -> Tā xǐ huàn tā zìjǐ -> 他喜欢自己

Zì jǐ can also be used to emphasize the subject similar to the English construction "I myself." or "he himself".

For example:

I myself like it. -> Wǒ zìjǐ xǐhuàn. -> 我自己喜欢

Chapter 9: Prepositions

Prepositions are words that precede nouns and pronouns to express place, time, objective, direction, reason, dependence, means, passivity, comparison, etc.

A preposition and its noun phrase form a prepositional phrase.

Prepositional phrases are commonly placed right before the verb and the object with the following sentence pattern:

Subject + Prepositional Phrase + Verb + Direct Object

Here are commonly used prepositions in Chinese:

Prepositions	Chinese	Meaning
bǎ	把	to hold
bèi	被	by
bǐ	比	particle used for comparison
chúle	除了	except for
còng	从	from
dào	到	until a certain

		time, to a place
duì	对	to (someone)
duìyú	对于	regarding
ēnjù	根据 g	based on
gěi	给	to, for
gēn	跟	with
guānyú	关于	concerning, about
wǎng	往	to, towards
wèile	为了	in order to
xiàng	向	towards
zài	在	in, on
tì	替	for (someone)
yòng	用	with

Verbs

There are three main types of verbs in Mandarin:

Action verbs

Modal verbs

Stative verbs

Action or Activity Verbs

Action verbs are words that denote activity or action. Chinese action verbs have time duration.

Here are some examples:

看 -> kàn -> to see

喝 -> hē -> to drink

吃 -> chī -> to eat

買/买 -> mǎi -> to buy

說/说 -> shuō -> to talk

Activity verbs occur over a time period which can be specified with verb suffixes. For instance, to indicate an ongoing action, you can use the verb suffix zhe 着. To indicate an action that's happening at the present moment, you can use the verb suffixes zhèng 正 or zhèngzài 正在. To indicate an action that happened in the past, the verb suffix le 了 can be used with action verbs.

Stative Verbs

Stative verbs are used to denote a relatively unchanging state and their primary function is to describe a noun. A joining word is used to link the noun to the description or stative verb. Stative verbs include dà (large), gāo (tall), and gùi (expensive) which are often translated as adjectives.

For instance, to express "he is tall" in Chinese, you will use "hěn" between "tā" (he) and "gāo" (tall). Hence, "he is tall" is "tā hěn gāo".

Auxiliary or Modal Verbs

Auxiliary verbs express necessity, willingness, obligation, possibility, or capability. They are placed before the main verbs and help indicate the mood or tone of the verb. Auxiliary verbs are the equivalent of "will", "should", and "can" in English.

Take note that if a sentence has an auxiliary verb, it is the auxiliary verb that gets modified and not the main verb. For instance, to negate a sentence, you will have to place the negation word before the auxiliary.

Auxiliary verbs can't take the aspect particles le 了, zhe 着, and (zhe), and guo 过. They can't be reduplicated, too.

The verb shì 是 (to be)

Shì, the Chinese equivalent of the verb "to be", is used differently in Mandarin. Shì 是 is used to connect nouns, pronouns, or noun phrases to indicate identity. It is commonly not used with adjectives.

The basic structure for linking nouns with "shì" is:

First Noun + shì 是 + Second Noun

Examples:

I am a student. -> wǒ shì xuéshēng -> 我 是 学生.

I am an American. -> wǒ shì měi guó rén -> 我 是 美 国 人。

I am a teacher. -> wǒ shì lǎoshī -> 我 是 老师。

Chapter 10: Expressing location with the verb zài (在)

General Locations

The verb zài (在) is used to express location or existence in a place. In English, you'll have to use the verb "to be" and a preposition to express location. In Chinese, all you need is the verb "zài" to express general locations.

Examples:

They are in England. -> Tāmen zài Yīngguó. -> 他们 在 英国

Who is in the bathroom? -> Shuí zài xǐshǒujiān? -> 谁 在 洗手间？

Are you at the office? -> Nǐ zài gōngsī ma? -> 你 在 公司 吗？

in the USA -> zài Měiguó -> 在 美国

in New York -> zài Niǔyuē -> 在 纽约

Specific Locations

To show a subject's specific location or a subject's location relative to another object, you'll use the construction "zài"(在) + Place + nouns of locality such as shàng 上, xià 下, (lǐ) 里, or pángbiān 旁边. When used at the beginning of a sentence, "zài"(在) becomes an optional character.

Examples:

He is downstairs. -> Tā zài lóu xià. -> 他 在 楼 下.

I'm in the train. -> Wǒ zài huǒchē shàng. -> 我 在 火车 里.

The verb jiào

The verb jiào (叫) is used to indicate a person's name or how someone or something is called.

You can give your name or someone else's name using jiào (叫) with the following structure:

Subject + jiào 叫 + Name

My name is Michael. -> Wǒ jiào Michael. -> 我 叫 Michael.

My brother's name is Carcl. -> Wǒ gēgē jiào Carl. ->我 哥哥 叫 Carl.

My boss is called Lǎo Mù. -> Wǒmen de lǎobǎn jiào Lǎo Mù. 我 们 的 老板 叫 老木.

My dog is called Spotty. -> Wǒ de gǒu jiào Spotty. 我 的 狗 叫 Spotty.

This beer is called Bud. -> Zhè zhǒng píjiǔ jiào Bud. 这 种 啤酒 叫 Bud.

You can also use jiào (叫) to ask for a person's name:

What's your name? -> Nǐ jiào shénme míngzì? -> 你 叫 什么 名 字？

The auxiliary verb yào 要

The auxiliary verb yào 要 has many uses. One is to express "be going to" which is used when discussing what you intend to do.

The basic structure for yào 要 in this usage is:

Subject + yào 要 + Verb

When using yào for this purpose, an expression to indicate time is typically required and may be placed in front of or after the subject.

I'm going to buy a television. -> Wǒ yào mǎi yī gè diànshì. -> 我 要 买 一 个 电视.

Are you guys going out? -> Nǐmen yào chūqù ma? -> 你们 要 出 去 吗？

Using néng 能 to express ability or possibility:

The verb néng 能 is used to indicate ability which is not formally or consciously studied or learned. When used in this context, it is translated as "can" in English.

The basic structure for this usage is:

Subject + néng 能 + Verb + Object

Examples:

I can eat 40 dumplings. -> Wǒ néng chī sìshí gè jiǎozi. -> 我 能 吃 四十 个 饺子

Using kěyǐ 可以 to express permission

The auxiliary verb kěyǐ 可以 is primarily used to express permission. It is best translated as "may" but you will often read it translated as "can".

The basic structure for using kěyǐ 可以 is as follows:

Subject + kěyǐ 可以 + Verb + Object

Examples:

May I come in? -> Wǒ kěyǐ jìnlái ma? -> 我 可以 进来 吗？

May we eat in the office? -> Wǒmen kěyǐ zài bàngōngshì chīfàn ma? -> 我们 可以 在 办公室 吃饭 吗?

Negating kěyǐ 可以

Sentences using kěyǐ 可以 are negated by inserting "bù" 不 before it.

The basic structure is:

Subject + bù 不 + kěyǐ 可以 + Verb + Object

Examples:

You can't smoke here. -> Zhèlǐ bù kěyǐ chōuyān. -> 这里 不 可以 抽烟。

We can't be late.-> Wǒmen dōu bù kěyǐ chídào. -> 我们 都 不 可 以 迟到

Chapter 11: Expressing something you want to do

The verb yào 要

The auxiliary verb yào 要 is used to express someone's desire to do something. The basic structure for this usage is:

Subject + yào 要 + Verb + Object

Examples:

He wants to study Chinese. -> Tā yào xué zhōngwén. -> 他 要 学 中文。

The baby wants to sleep. -> Bǎobao yào shuìjiào. -> 宝宝 要 睡觉。

The verb xiǎng 想

Instead of yào 要, another way to express what you want to do is by using the auxiliary verb xiǎng 想. These verbs are almost always interchangeable. The difference is yào 要 is used when you are stating something that you actually need or want to do. Xiǎng 想, on the other hand, is mosty used to express an idea of what you want to do or something that you need not take action on. It is closer to the English phrase "would like to".

Examples:

I would like to drink coffee. -> Wǒ xiǎng hē kāfēi. -> 我 想 喝 咖 啡。

What would you like to eat? -> Nǐ xiǎng chī shénme? -> 你 想 吃 什么？

Expressing future action with huì 会

The auxiliary verb huì 会 has many uses. One of this is to indicate that something will occur or that someone will take an action.

The structure for this usage is:

Subject + huì 会 + Verb + Object

Examples:

Tomorrow, I will eat out. -> Míngtiān wǒ huì zài wàimian chīfàn. -> 明天 我 会 在 外面 吃饭。

We won't tell him. -> Wǒmen bù huì gàosu nǐ. -> 我们不会 告诉 他。

Will it rain tomorrow? -> Míngtiān huì xiàyǔ ma? -> 明天 会 下 雨 吗？

Will the boss agree? -> Lǎobǎn huì tóngyì ma? -> 老板 会 同意 吗？

Standard Negation with bù 不

Negating Verbs

In Chinese, verbs are generally negated by placing bù 不 before the verb. The basic structure is:

Subject + bù 不 + + Verb + Object

Examples:

I don't want to work today. -> Wǒ jīntiān bù xiǎng gōngzuò. -> 我 今天 不 想 工作。

Don't you like me? -> Nǐ bù xǐhuan wǒ ma? -> 你 不 喜欢 我 吗？

Almost any verb can be negated by placing bù 不 in front of the verb with the exception of yǒu (有) which is negated by méi 没. In addition, you can't use bù 不 when talking about a past action.

Negating Adjectives

To negate adjectives with bù 不, you'll use the same structure as when negating with verbs:

Subject + bù 不 + Adjective

This is not expensive. -> Zhè ge bù guì. -> 这 个 不 贵。

I'm not hungry. -> Wǒ bù è. -> 我 不 饿。

Our company is not big. -> Wǒmen gōngsī bù dà. -> 我们 公司 不 大。

Negating the verb yǒu 有

The verb yǒu 有 is the only verb that is negated differently. Instead of bù 不, you will use méi 没 to negate this verb which is translated as "have" in English. Here is the basic structure:

Subject + méi 没 + yǒu 有 + Object

I don't have any questions. -> Wǒ méi yǒu wèntí. -> 我 没 有 问题。

Does he not have a job? -> Tā méi yǒu gōngzuò ma? -> 他 没 有 工作 吗？

We don't have money . -> Wǒmen méi yǒu qián. -> 我们没 有 钱.

I don't have time. -> Wǒ méi yǒu shíjiān. -> 我 没有 时间。

Negating past actions

While habitual or present actions are negated with bù 不, past actions are negated with méiyǒu 没有 to express something that wasn't done or didn't happen.

The basic structure is:

Subject + méiyǒu 没有 / méi 没 + Verb

Examples:

They didn't speak. -> Tāmen méiyǒu shuōhuà. -> 他们 没有 说话。

I didn't go to work. -> Wǒ méiyǒu qù shàngbān. -> 我 没有 去上班。

I didn't eat breakfast. -> Wǒ méiyǒu chī zǎofàn. -> 我 没有 吃早饭。

Activity Verbs

English Verb	Pinyin	Chinese
announce	xuān bù	宣布
bounce	tántiào	弹跳
brush	shuā	刷
build	jiànzào	建造

call	dǎdiànhuà	打电话
carry	ná	拿
catch	zhuāzhù	抓住
choose	xuǎn	选
clean	dá sǎo	打扫
climb	pá	爬
close	guān	关
cold	zé mà	责骂
color	túsè	涂色
comb	shū	梳
cook	pēng rèn	烹饪
crawl	pá xíng	爬行
cry	kū	哭
dance	tiào wǔ	跳舞
dig	wā	挖
dive	tiàoshuǐ	跳水
drag	tuō	拖
draw	huà	画
dream	zuómèng	做梦
drop	diào luò	掉落

dry	chuī gān	吹干
eat	chī	吃
fall	luò xià	落下
feed	wèi	喂
fly	fēi	飞
hit	dǎ	打
hold	ná	拿
hop	tiào yuè	跳跃
itch	yǎng	痒
jump	tiào	跳
kick	tī	踢
kneel	guì	跪
lean	kào	靠
leap	tiào guò	跳过
lift	tái	抬
look	kàn	看
open	kāi	开
pick up	jiǎn	捡
play	wán	玩
pull	lā	拉

punch	quánjī	拳击
push	tuī	推
run	pǎo	跑
see	jù	锯
shake hands	wò shǒu	握手
sit	zuò	坐
talk	jiāo tán	交谈
throw	rēng	扔
tiptoe	diàn jiǎo zǒu	垫脚走
feel dizzy	tóu yūn	头晕
walk	zǒu	走
watch	kàn	看
whistle	chuī kǒu shào	吹口哨
wink	zhá yǎn	眨眼

Chapter 12: Adverbs

Adverbs are used to indicate degree, extent, time, logical functions, probability, negation, etc. Chinese adverbs usually come at the start of the predicate before a verb phrase, adjective, or a preposition phrase. Here is a common sentence pattern with an adverb:

Subject + Adverbs + Predicate (Verb Phrase/Adjective/Prepositional Phrase)

To say, "She likes cats very much":

Tā -> fēicháng -> xǐhuān -> māo.

她 -> 非常 -> 喜欢 -> 猫。

She -> very much -> likes -> cats.

Using the adverb hěn 很 with Adjectives

The adverb hěn 很 may be used to link a noun to an adjective and form a simple sentence with the following structure:

Noun + hěn 很 + Adjective

The sentence is translated as "Noun is Adjective".

Examples:

Chinese is difficult. -> Zhōngwén hěn nán -> 中文很难。

I'm good. -> Wǒ hěn hǎo. -> 我 很 好。

She is happy. -> Tā hěn gāoxìng. -> 她很 高兴。

You are pretty. -> Nǐ hěn piàoliang. -> 你 很 漂亮。

Commonly used Chinese adverbs:

Adverbs	Chinese	Meaning
cái	才	only, only then
dàgài	大概	approximate
dāng chū	当初	originally, at that time
dōu	都	all
fēicháng	非常	extremely, very much
góu	够	enough
hěn	很	very
jiāngyào	将要	will, shall
jīhū	几乎	almost

jīng cháng	经常	frequently
kěn dìng	肯定	sure
kěnéng	可能	maybe
tài	太	very, too much
uóxǔ	或许 h	perhaps, maybe
yīdìng	一定	surely, certainly
yǐjīng	已经	already
zhǐ	只	only
zuìhóu	最后	finally

Particles

Particles are function words that stand for nothing on their own. These Chinese words depend on other words to give meaning and always maintain a neutral tone. Particles have many functions depending on the context it is in. They can indicate time, mood, voice, relationship, etc.

Common Particles

le 了

The particle le 了 can be used as an aspect particle to modify verbs when placed after it or as a modal particle when placed at the end of a sentence.

de 的

De 的 is a structural particle which indicates that the word preceding it has an attributive function. It is used to show possession and associate an adjective to a noun.

ma 吗

The particle ma 吗 is used for asking Yes-No questions and forming tag questions.

ne 呢

The particle ne 呢 is used for asking reciprocal questions as well as simple questions.

Chapter 13: Adjectives

Chinese adjectives differ from their English adjectives because they also function as verbs and are called stative verbs. When a noun is modified by an adjective, the term "de" 的, an associate particle, is used to link both words.

Chinese adjectives have the following characteristics:

- Adjectives generally function as predicates, complements, or attributes.

- Most adjectives can be modified by the adverbs "不" and "很".

- Adjectives can be reduplicated to emphasize the quality of the word they describe.

dà -> 大 (big)

xiǎo -> 小 (small)

kuài -> 快 (fast)

màn -> 慢 (slow)

cháng -> 长 (long)

duǎn -> 短 (short)

yuǎn -> 远 (far)

jìn -> 近 (close)

yě -> 也 (also)

Single-character words that are placed before a noun become adjectives on their own. For example, 小手 xiǎo shǒu means "small hand". The particle de 的 can also be added between the single-character word and the noun to be modified. Hence, 小的手 xiǎode shǒu means small hand.

You can repeat the single-character word and add the character de 的 to emphasize the quality it describes. For example, to indicate very small hands, you'll say, "xiǎoxiǎo de shǒu" 小小的手.

You can do the same with two-character words to emphasize quality but you'll have to repeat each character individually. For instance, a two-character word for pretty can be used to describe a girl with 漂亮的女孩 (piàoliang de nǔhái) or pretty girl. To emphasize on the quality being described, you can repeat each character and say "漂漂亮亮的女孩 (piāo piàoliang liàng de nǔhái) to mean very pretty girl.

Using huòzhě 或者 to give options

In English, you would normally use "or" when presenting or considering options. It is also used in "either-or" constructions. In Chinese, this function is performed by huòzhě 或者 using the following structure:

Option 1 + huòzhě 或者 + Option 2

Take note that huòzhě 或者 is used as "or" only in statements. Another word, háishì 还是 is used as "or" in questions.

Example:

Saturday or Sunday are both okay. Xīngqīliù huòzhě xīngqītiān, dōu kěyǐ. 星期六 或者 星期天 都 可以。

Chapter 14: Forming Sentences

Mandarin verbs are not affected by time or person. This means that verbs have no tenses and that they have the same form for plural or singular subjects. Oftentimes, the only way to identify the subject or the object in a sentence is through the word order. This makes word order critical in Chinese sentences.

Subject + verb structure

The most basic word order in Chinese is subject + verb. You can practically form a sentence using only two words with this pattern.

Examples:

Subject -> Verb -> English

Wǒ -> dú. -> I read.

我 -> 读

Wǒ -> chī. -> I eat.

我 -> 吃

Wǒ -> shuō. -> I speak.

我 -> 说

Wǒ men -> chī. -> We eat.

我们 -> 吃.

Háizi -> dú. -> Children read.

孩子 -> 读.

Subject + Verb + Object

A Chinese sentence normally has an object and follows the same basic sentence S-V-O pattern used in English.

Examples:

Subject -> Verb -> Object

Wǒ -> shuō -> Zhōngwén. -> I speak Chinese.

我 -> 说 -> 中文

Tā -> chī -> ròu. -> He eats meat.

他 -> 吃 -> 肉

Tā -> hē -> chá ma? -> Does he drink tea?

他 -> 喝 -> 茶 吗？

Wǒ -> hē -> kā fēi. -> I drink coffee.

我 -> 喝 -> 咖 啡

Adding More Information to Basic Sentences

Placement of time phrases

Time words are usually placed immediately after the subject and always before the verb. You'll see them occasionally at the start of a sentence but never at the end.

Examples:

Wǒ-> měi -> tiān -> hē -> kā fēi. -> I drink coffee every day.

我 -> 每 -> 天 -> 喝 -> 咖 啡

I -> every day -> drink -> coffee

Míng tiān -> wǒ -> yào kàn -> zhè -> běn shū. -> Tomorrow, I will read this book.

明天 -> 我 -> 要看 -> 這本書

Tomorrow -> I -> will read -> this book.

When the time phrase has several constituents, the word order is from the biggest to the smallest time block.

For example, to say "8 o'clock last night", the word order would be:

zuó -> tiān -> wǎn -> shàng -> bā -> diǎn zhōng

昨-> 天-> 晚 -> 上 -> 八 -> 点 -> 钟

Placement of location phrase

The location phrase always comes before the verb and most commonly after the time phrase.

Examples:

at the library -> zài tú shū guǎn -> 在 图书馆

in the USA -> zài Měiguó -> 在 美国

Placement of Duration Phrases

A duration phrase is a time phrase that indicates how long an action happens. Chinese duration phrases do not require prepositions and are placed directly after the verb.

For example, to express "He was sick for two days":

Subject -> Verb -> Duration

Tā -> bìng -> le -> liǎng -> tiān

他 -> 病 -> 了 -> 两 -> 天

He -> sick -> two days

Chapter 15: Asking Questions in Mandarin

Asking questions in Mandarin is one of the things you need to learn. Here are basic question words you can use:

English	Pinyin	Chinese
Who?	Shuí?	谁？
Where?	Nǎlǐ?	哪里？
When?	Shénme shíhòu?	什么时候？
What?	Shénme?	什么？
Why?	Wèishéme?	为什么？
How?	Duōshǎo?	多少？
Can you?	Nǐ néng?	你能？
Would you?	Nǐ huì?	你会？
For how long?	Duōjiǔ?	多久？

Examples:

Who is he/she? -> Tā/tā shì shuí? -> 他/她是谁？

What's the time? -> Xiànzài jǐ diǎn zhōng? -> 现在几点钟？

Where's the bathroom? -> Xǐshǒujiān zài nǎlǐ? -> 洗手间在哪里？

Asking Yes-No Questions with ma 吗

You can easily form Yes-No questions in Mandarin by placing the question particle ma 吗 at the end of a statement. Practically any statement can be converted into a question by using this structure:

statement + ma 吗 ?

Examples:

Statement -> Yes-No Question

Nǐ huì zhōngwén. -> 你会中文。 -> Nǐ huì zhōngwén ma? 你会中文吗？

You speak Chinese. -> Do you speak Chinese?

Tā shì lǎobǎn. -> 他 是 老板。 -> Tā shì lǎobǎn ma? -> 他 是 老板 吗？

He is the boss. -> Is he the boss?

Nǐ xǐhuan kāfēi. -> 你 喜欢 咖啡。 -> Nǐ xǐhuan kāfēi ma? 你 喜欢 咖啡 吗？

You like coffee. -> Do you like coffee?

Nǐ shì dàxuéshēng. -> 你 是 大 学生 。 -> Nǐ shì dàxuéshēng ma? -> 你 是 学生 吗？

You are a college student. -> Are you a college student?

Zhè shì nǐ de. -> 这是你的。 -> Zhè shì nǐ de ma? -> 这是你的吗？

This is yours. -> Is this yours?

Nà shì fēijī. -> 那是飞机。 -> Nà shì fēijī ma? -> 那是飞机吗？

That is a plane. -> Is that a plane?

Forming tag questions with ma 吗

Besides constructing Yes-No questions, you can also use ma 吗 to form tag questions in Chinese. Tag questions are commonly used when asking for confirmation. This is the equivalent of "right", "isn't it", or "doesn't he?" in English. Besides conveying a request for information, adding ma 吗 helps soften a suggestion. To do this, you will have to use a confirmation word before adding ma 吗 at the end of the sentence. Words like 对 (duì), 可以 (kěyǐ), 是 (shì), and 好 (hǎo) may be placed in front of 吗 (ma) to form a tag question.

Examples:

You've met, right? -> Nǐmen jiànguo, duì ma? -> 你们 见过，对 吗？

Don't tell him, okay? -> Bú yào gàosù tā, hǎo ma? -> 不要 告诉 他， 好 吗？

Forming tag questions with bù 不

You can also form tag questions by placing an affirmative-negative question using bù 不 at the end of the sentence.

Here's the pattern:

Verb + bù 不 + Verb

Example:

Let's have coffee, okay? -> Wǒmen hē kāfēi, hǎo bu hǎo? -> 我们 喝咖啡，好不好?

Forming questions with ne 呢

You can use the particle ne 呢 to form reciprocal questions or ask questions like "how about" or "what about". You'll just have to put "ne" at the end of a topic or sentence.

Here's a classic example:

A: Nǐ hǎo ma? -> 你 好 吗？ -> How are you?

B: Wǒ hěn hǎo, nǐ ne? -> 我 很 好, 你 呢？ -> I'm fine, and you?

A: Wǒ yě hěn hǎo. -> 我 也 很 好。 -> I am fine, too.

Other Examples:

I'm home. What about you? -> Wǒ zài jiā. Nǐ ne? -> 我 在 家. 你 呢 ？

I'm busy. How about you? -> Wǒ hěn máng. Nǐ ne? -> 我很忙.你呢?

Chapter 16: Making Comparisons

Basic Comparisons with bǐ 比

A common way to compare things in Chinese is by using bǐ 比 to express "than" in English. To express that the first noun has more of the quality described, the basic structure is:

Noun 1 + bǐ 比 + Noun 2 + Adjective

Examples:

He is older than the teacher. -> Tā bǐ lǎoshī dà. -> 他 比 老师 大 。

You are smarter than me. -> Nǐ bǐ wǒ cōngming. -> 你 比 我 聪 明 。

Basic comparisons with "méiyǒu" 没有

Another way to make comparisons in Chinese is by using méiyǒu 没有 to express that something is "not as" good as the other in terms of the quality indicated. The basic structure is:

Noun1 + meiyou 没有 + Noun2 + Adjective

Huǒchē méiyǒu fēijī kuài.　火车 没有 飞机 快。Trains aren't as fast as airplanes.

Pīnyīn méiyǒu hànzì nán.　拼音 没有 汉字 难。Pinyin is not as difficult as Chinese characters.

Expressing Comparison with yīyàng 一样

To express that two things are equal in some way, you can place the word yīyàng 一样 at the end of the sentence.

Here is the basic structure for comparison with yīyàng 一样

Noun 1 + gēn 跟 / hé 和 + Noun 2 + 一样

Examples:

Tā de xìnggé gēn tā bàba yīyàng.

她的 性格 跟她爸爸一样。

She has the same personality as her dad.

Using yīyàng 一样 with Adjectives

To express that the first noun has the same quality as the second noun, you can add an adjective after yīyàng 一样.

Structure:

Noun 1 + gēn 跟 / hé 和 + Noun 2 + 一样 + adjective

Examples:

Tā hé tāgēge yīyàng gāo.

她 和 她哥哥 一样 高。

She is as tall as her older brother.

Expressing much more in comparisons

If you want to emphasize or increase the intensity of your comparisons, you can use one of the equivalents of "much more" in Mandarin — duō/duō le/hěn duō. Here's the basic structure:

Subject + 比 + Noun + Adjective + 得多 / 多了 / 很多

Examples:

She is a lot taller than I am. -> Tā bǐ wǒ gāo dé duō -> 她 比 我 高 得多。

Expressing the superlative with zuì 最

The most common way to express the superlative in Chinese is by using zuì 最 in front of the adjective.

Chinese language is the most difficult. -> Hànyǔ zuì nán. -> 汉语 最 难。

the slowest -> zuì màn de -> 最慢的

the richest -> zuì fùyǒu de -> 最富有的

Chapter 17: Chinese in Action

Introducing Yourself

Learning how to introduce yourself is one of the basic steps in learning a new language. In this chapter, you will learn common phrases to introduce yourself and meet new people.

To introduce yourself and say something about you, you will find these phrases handy:

My name is Paul. -> wǒ jiào Paul -> 我 叫 Paul.

I'm 25 years old. -> wǒ èr shí wǔ suì. -> 我二十五岁.

I live in New York. -> wǒ zhù zài Niǔyuē -> 我 住 在在 纽约

I'm an American. -> wǒ shì měiguó rén -> 我是美国人

I'm single. -> wǒ dānshēn -> 我单身。

I'm a teacher. -> wǒ shì yī míng jiàoshī -> 我是一名教師

Here are some questions that may be asked of you when you're in a Mandarin-speaking place. Learn them and try to use them in your daily conversations:

May I know your name? -> Nín guì xìng? -> 您 贵 姓?

What is your name? -> Nǐ jiào shénme míngzì? -> 你叫什么名字?

How old are you? -> Nǐ duōdà niánjì? -> 你多大年纪？

Are you married? -> Nǐ jiéhūnle ma? -> 你结婚了吗？

Where do you live? -> Nǐ zhù zài nǎlǐ? -> 你住在哪里？

Do you have children? -> Nǐ yǒu háizi ma? -> 你有孩子吗？

Do you speak Chinese? -> Nǐ jiǎng zhōngwén ma? -> 你讲中文吗？

What kind of work do you do? -> Nǐ zuò shénme gōngzuò? -> 你做什么工作？

What is the weather like today? -> Jīntiān tiānqì zěnme yàng? -> 今天天气怎么？

Addressing people in Chinese

Chinese has a different way of introducing and addressing people. You will have to say the surname before the title. Family names come first before given names.

You may use the following common titles when addressing people in Chinese:

Mr. -> xiānshēng -> 先生

Mrs. ->tài tai -> 太太

Miss/Ms. -> nǚ shì -> 女士

To address Miss Zhuo, for example, you can say Zhuó nǚ shì in Chinese.

To address professionals, you would usually state the profession after the family name.

For instance, to address, lawyer Wang, you might say 'Wang Lu Shi'.

Talking About Your Family

Your family is an important part of your life and talking about them is one of the natural progressions when learning a new language. Here are key phrases you can use to talk about your family:

This is my father. -> Zhè shì wǒ bàba. -> 这是我爸爸。

This is my mother. -> Zhè shì wǒ māma. -> 这是我妈妈。

This is my wife. -> Zhè shì wǒ tàitai. ->这是我太太。

This is my son. -> Zhè shì wǒ érzi. -> 这是我儿子。

This is my (younger) brother. -> Zhè shì wǒ dìdi. -> 这是我弟弟。

I have a son. -> Wǒ yǒu yí ge érzi. -> 我有一个儿子。

My father is a doctor. -> Wǒ bàba shì yīsheng. -> 我爸爸 是 医生。

He is my elder brother. -> Tā shì wǒde gēge. -> 他是我的哥哥。

Members of the Family:

Father	bàba	爸爸
Mother	māma	妈妈
Elder brother	gēge	哥哥

Younger brother	dìdi	弟弟
Elder sister	jiějie	姐姐
Younger sister	mèimei	妹妹
Son	érzi	儿子
Daughter	nǔ'ér	女儿
Son's wife	xífù	媳妇
Daughter's husband	nǔxù	女婿
Elder brother	gēge	哥哥
Younger brother	dìdi	弟弟
Elder sister	jiějie	姐姐
Younger sister	mèimei	妹妹
Grandson	sūnzi	孙子
Granddaughter	sūnnǔ	孙女
Paternal grandfather	yéye	爷爷
Paternal grandmother	nǎinai	奶奶
Maternal grandfather	wàigōng	外公
Maternal grandmother	wàipó	外婆
Father's elder brother	bóbo	伯伯
Father's younger brother	shūshu	叔叔
Father's elder/younger	gūgu	姑姑

sister		
Mother's elder/younger brother	jiùjiu	舅舅
Mother's elder/younger sister	yímā	姨妈
Grandson's wife	sūnxífù	孙媳妇
Granddaughter's husband	sūnnǔxù	孙女婿

Chapter 18: Eating Out

Eating out is one of the pleasures of travelling. Chinese cuisines are delectable and known worldwide and you will likely take the opportunity to dine at local restaurants when you're on a visit. You may want to learn important phrases and words for ordering food and drinks in a restaurant.

Dining out in Chinese restaurants is actually simpler and straightforward because you won't have to bother about polite words and other formalities.

To call the waiter's attention:

Fú wù yuán! diǎn cài! -> 服务员！点菜！ Waiter, we'd like to order food!

To ask for the menu:

Qǐng bǎ càidān gěi wǒ -> 请把菜单给我 -> Please give me the menu.

The waiter may also ask you for your order:

Nǐ xiǎng yàodiǎn shénme? -> What would you like to order?

你想要点什么？

Nǐ xiǎng hē diǎn shénme? -> What would you like to drink?

你想喝点什么？

Nǐ xiǎng yào jǐ bēi? -> Have many bottles would you like?

你想要几杯？

Nín yàodiǎn shénme? -> What would you like?

您要点儿什么？

To make your order:

wǒ yào____ -> 我要_____ -> I want_____

More often, you will need measure words to order your food. You can use fèn 份 which means a dish/an order or pán 盘 to order a plate of something. For rice or noodles, you'll use wǎn 碗 whch means "bowl."

For drinks, you may use the following measure words:

píng -> 瓶 -> bottle

tīng -> 听 -> can

hú -> 壺 -> pot

bēi -> 杯 -> glass/cup

Here are drinks you might see on the menu:

Pinyin	Chinese	English
chá	茶	Tea
lǜ chá	綠茶	Green tea
hóng chá	紅茶	Black tea
wūlóng chá	烏龍茶	Oolong tea
niú nǎi	牛奶	Milk
kāfēi	咖啡	Coffee
hēi kāfēi	黑咖啡	Black coffee

nǎi jīng	奶精	Cream
táng	糖	Sugar
bù jiā táng	不加糖	No sugar
bàn táng	半糖	Half sugar
guǒ zhī	果汁	Juice
liǔchéng zhī	柳橙汁	Orange juice
píngguǒ zhī	蘋果汁	Apple juice
fènglí zhī	鳳梨汁	Pineapple juice
xīguā zhī	西瓜汁	Watermelon juice
níngméng zhī	檸檬汁	Lemonade
bīng	冰	Ice
yǐn liào	飲料	Soft drinks
kělè	可樂	Cola
kāi shuǐ	開水	Water
kuàng quán shuǐ	礦泉水	Mineral water
bīng shuǐ	冰水	Ice water
píjiǔ	啤酒	Beer
jiǔ dān	酒單	Wine list
pútáo jiǔ	葡萄酒	Wine

xiāng bīn	香檳	Champagne
hóng jiǔ	紅酒	Red Wine
bái jiǔ	白酒	White wine
qìpāo jiǔ	氣泡酒	Sparkling wine

For food, you might want to order any of the following:

Pinyin	Chinese	English
Zǎocān	早餐	Breakfast
Wǔcān	午餐	Lunch
Wǎncān	晚餐	Dinner
Língshí	零食	Snack
niúròu	牛肉	beef
jīròu	鸡肉	chicken
Yáng pái	羊排	Lamb chops
Kǎo niúròu	烤牛肉	Roast beef
Nǎilào hànbǎo	奶酪汉堡	Cheeseburger
Shǔ piàn	薯片	Crisps
Zhà shǔ tiáo	炸薯条	French fries
Règǒu	热狗	Hot dog

Yángcōng quān	洋葱圈	Onion rings
Bǐsàbǐng	比萨饼	Pizza
Ròu jiàng yì fěn	肉酱意粉	Spaghetti Bolognese
Sānmíngzhì	三明治	Sandwich
Shālā	沙拉	Salad

To make special requests:

Wǒ bù xǐhuān là de -> I don't like spicy foods.

我不喜欢辣的

wǒ chī sù de -> I'm a vegetarian.

我吃素的

Wǒ bù chī zhūròu -> I don't eat pork.

我不吃猪肉

Wǒ bú yào wèi jīng -> I don't want MSG.

我不要味精

Complaints you might have:

Wǒ méiyǒu diǎn zhège -> I didn't order this.

我没有点这个

Zhè cài liáng le -> This dish is cold.

这菜凉了

Qián bùduì -> The bill is wrong.

钱不对

To ask for your bill:

Qǐng héduì -> The check, please.

请核对

Restaurant terms:

Kuàizi	筷子	Chopsticks
Gēngchí	羹匙	Spoon

Cān dāo	餐刀	Knife
Cān chā	餐叉	Fork
Chábēi	茶杯	Cup
Pánzi	盘子	Plate
Wǎn	碗	Bowl
Cānjīn	餐巾	Napkin

Chapter 19: Asking for Directions

Asking for and comprehending directions are practical skills that any traveler should learn.

One of the simplest way to ask for the location of a place is to use the question word "where".

Nǐ zài nǎlǐ?	你在哪里？	Where are you?
Yínháng zài nǎlǐ?	银行在哪里？	Where is the bank?
Yóujú zài nǎlǐ er?	邮局在哪里儿？	Where is the post office?
Nǐ zài nǎlǐ?	你在哪里？	Where are you?

To ask for direction, you can begin with the phrase "Wǒ zěnme qù__" which means "How do I get to__"

Wǒ zěnme qù _____ -> How do I get to_____

我怎么去___？

Wǒ rúhé zěnme qù yínháng ne? -> How do I get to the bank?

我如何怎么去银行呢？

Wǒ zěnme rúhé qù jīchǎng? -> How do I get to the airport?

我怎么如何去机场？

Wǒ zěnme dào huǒchē zhàn? -> How do I get to the train station?

我怎么到火车站？

Tā shì jìn ma? -> 它是近吗？ -> Is it near?

Tā yuǎn ma? -> 它远吗？ -> Is it far?

Places to see:

Pinyin	Chinese	English
jī chǎng	机场	airport
yín háng	银行	bank
qiáo	桥	Bridge
gōng jiāo zhàn	公交站	Bus station
kā fēi ba	咖啡吧	Cafe
mǎ xì tuán	马戏团	Circus
xiāo fáng jú	消防局	Fire station
jiā yóu	加油站	Gas station

zhàn		
zá huò diàn	杂货店	Grocery store
yī yuàn	医院	Hospital
fáng zi	房子	House
wū zi	屋子	House
xiǎo wū	小屋	Hut
dǎo	岛	Island
dēng tǎ	灯塔	Lighthouse
bó wù guǎn	博物馆	Museum
bàn gōng lóu	办公楼	Office building
gōng diàn	宫殿	Palace
chǒng wù diàn	宠物店	Pet shop
yóu jú	邮局	Post office
jiān yù	监狱	Prison
mó tiān dà lóu	摩天大楼	Restaurant
fàn diàn	饭店	Restaurant
shāng diàn	商店	Shopping mall
mó tiān dà lóu	摩天大楼	Skyscraper

chāo shì	超市	Supermarket
tǎ	塔	Tower
huǒ chē zhàn	火车站	Train station

Useful Phrases:

jiē -> 街; lù 路 -> street

zuǒbiān zhuǎnwān -> 左边转弯 -> Turn left.

zuǒguǎi -> 左拐 -> Turn left.

yòubiān zhuǎnwān -> 右边转弯 -> Turn right.

yòuguǎi -> 右拐 -> Turn right.

yìzhízǒu -> 一直走 -> Go straight.

dàole -> 到了 -> I've reached my destination.

diàotóu -> 掉头 -> U-turn

zuǒbiān -> 左边 -> left

yòubiān -> 右边 -> right

wǎngqián zǒu -> 往前走 -> straight ahead

běi -> 北 -> north

nán -> 南 -> south

dōng -> 东 -> east

xī -> 西 -> west

Miànqián -> 面前 -> front

Hòu bèibù -> 后背部 -> back

Lǐmiàn -> 里面 -> inside

Wàimiàn -> 外面 -> outside

Yǐshàng miàn -> 以上面 -> above

Xiàmiàn -> 下面 -> below

Xiàngshàng -> 向上 -> up

Xiàng xià -> 向下 -> down

Xiāngfǎn -> 相反 -> opposite

Pángbiān -> 旁边 -> next to

Dōngnán -> 东南 -> southeast

Xīnán -> 西南 -> southwest

Dōngběi -> 东北 -> northeast

Xīběi -> 西北 -> northwest

Chapter 20: Shopping

When you're visiting a foreign country, you will probably end up shopping for clothes, gifts, souvenirs, or groceries. You might want to go to malls, department stores, art shops, night markets, and supermarkets. You need the right words to buy, haggle, and get the items you want.

Here are key phrases you can use when shopping in a Mandarin-speaking place:

duōshǎo qián? -> 多少钱？-> How much is this?

tài guì le -> 太贵了。-> That's too expensive.

Nǐ néng jiàngjià ma? -> 你能降价吗？ -> Can you lower the price?

wo fu bu qi -> 我付不起。-> I can't afford it.

wǒ bù yào -> 我不要。-> I don't want it.

wǒ méiyǒu xìngqù -> 我没有兴趣。-> I'm not interested.

wǒ yào mǎi zhège -> 我要买这个。-> I'll take it.

Tā bù shìhé -> 它不适合 -> It doesn't fit.

yǒu méiyǒu wǒde chǐcùn? -> 有没有我的尺寸？ -> Do you have this in my size?

Wǒ xiǎng tuì kuǎn -> 我想退款 -> I want a refund.

Wǒ xiǎng tuìhuò -> 我想退货 -> I would like to return this.

Nǐ shōu ná xìnyòngkǎ ma? -> 你收拿信用卡吗？ -> Do you take credit cards?

qǐng gěi wǒ dàizi -> 请给我袋子。-> Please give me a bag.

Shopping for supplies/grocery items:

(wǒ yào _____) -> 我要_____ -> I need ____

féizào -> 肥皂 -> soap

xǐfàjīng -> 洗发精 -> shampoo

yágāo -> 牙膏 -> toothpaste

yáshuā -> 牙刷 -> toothbrush

wèishēng miántiáo -> 卫生棉条 -> tampons

gǎnmào yào -> 感冒药 -> cold medicine

zhèntòngjì -> 镇痛剂 -> pain relievers

wèicháng yào -> 胃肠药 -> stomach medicine

yǔsǎn -> 雨伞 -> an umbrella

fángshàiyó -> 防晒油 -> sunblock lotion

diànchí -> 电池 -> batteries

tìdāo -> 剃刀 -> razor

yóupiào -> 邮票 -> postage stamps

míngxìnpiàn -> 明信片 -> postcard

zhǐ -> 纸 -> writing paper

qiānbǐ -> 铅笔 -> pencil

bǐ -> 笔 -> pen

yǎnjìng -> 眼镜 -> glasses

Useful Shopping Terms

Pinyin	Chinese	English
Shūdiàn	书店	Bookstore
Fúzhuāng diàn	服装店	Clothes shop
Bǎihuò shāngdiàn	百货商店	Department store
Yàodiàn	药店	Drug store
Lǐpǐn diàn	礼品店	Gift shop
Wǔjīn diàn	五金店	Hardware store
Zhūbǎo diàn	珠宝店	Jewellery store

Chàngpiàn diàn	唱片店	Record store
Xié diàn	鞋店	Shoe store
Chāoshì	超市	Supermarket
Wánjù diàn	玩具店	Toy store
Yī lóu	一楼	First floor
Èr lóu	二楼	Second floor
Sān lóu	三楼	Third floor
Sì lóu	四楼	Fourth Floor
Wǔ lóu	五楼	Fifth floor
Diàntī	电梯	Elevator
Shānghù	商户	Merchandise
Shòuhuòyuán	售货员	Salesperson

Getting Around

To get to your destinations, you will likely take public transportation. You'll need to learn important Mandarin phrases to make travelling easier and more fun.

Taking a Taxi

When taking a taxi, you have to know how to give directions. Here are some useful phrases:

chū zū chē! -> 出租车 -> Taxi!

qǐng kāidào _____ -> 请开到_____。 -> Take me to _____, please.

qǐng dào zhèi jiā fàndiàn -> 请到这家饭店 -> To this hotel, please.

tōngguò -> 通过 -> to pass

shàng wǎng shàng zǒu shēng -> 上往上走升 -> to go up

wǎng xià zǒu -> 往下走 -> to go down

yòu zhuǎn -> 右转 -> Turn right.

zuǒ zhuǎn -> 左转 -> Turn left.

yīzhí wǎng qián zǒu -> 一直往前走 -> Go straight ahead.

diàotóu niǔzhuǎn -> 掉头扭转 -> Turn around.

huíqù -> 回去 -> Go back.

sījī -> 司机 -> taxi driver

Riding Buses and Trains

qù___ de piào duō shǎo qián?   How much is a ticket to _____?

去____的票多少钱

qù bù qù ____ -> Do you go to _____

去不去____

Jǐdiǎn kāi/dào -> What time does it leave/arrive?

几点开/到

dānchéng/ fǎnwǎng piào -> single/return ticket

单程/返往票

chē -> 车 -> vehicle (train, bus, or taxi)

xínglǐ -> 行李 -> luggage

Train preferences:

yìngzuò -> 硬座 -> hard seat

yìngwò -> 硬卧 -> hard sleeper

ruǎnzuò -> 软座 -> soft seat

ruǎnwò -> 软卧 -> soft sleeper

Finding a Place to Stay

When it comes to accommodations, travelers have different needs and preferences. Whether you want to stay in a luxurious hotel or in a place with the most basic features, you have to know important Mandarin phrases.

Finding accommodations

Depending on your preferences or budget, you'll have several options when looking for a place to stay. Here are the most common types of accommodations you can expect:

bīnguǎn/jiǔdiàn -> 宾馆/酒店 -> hotel

lǚguǎn -> 旅馆 -> hostel/cheap hotel

duōrénfáng -> 多人房 -> dormitory

dānrénfáng -> 单人房 -> single room

shuāngrénfáng -> 双人房 -> twin room

háohuá tàofáng -> 豪华套房 -> deluxe suite

biāozhǔn fángjiān -> 标准房 -> standard room

pǔtōngfáng -> 普通房 -> economy room

Booking a Hotel

Nǐmen yǒu fángjiān ma? -> 你们有房间吗？ -> Is there a vacant room?

Wǒ dǎsuàn zhù ___ yè. -> 我打算住____夜。 -> I will stay for ____ nights.

Yǒu méiyǒu____ -> 有没有___ -> Does the room come with____

___chuángdān? -> ___床单？ -> ___bedsheets?

___yùshì? -> ___.浴室？ -> ___a bathroom?

___diànhuà? -> ___电话？ -> ___a telephone

___diànshì？ -> ___电视？ -> ___a TV?

___kōng tiáo -> ___空 调 -> ___air conditioning

Nǐmen yǒu méiyǒu bǎoxiǎn xiāng? -> 你们有没有保险箱？ -> Do you have a safe?

Wǒ xiànzài yào zǒu. -> 我现在要走。-> I want to check out.

Chapter 21: Vocabulary Lists

Fruits:

píng guǒ	苹果	apple
xìng	杏	apricot
xiāng jiāo	香蕉	banana
gān zhè	甘蔗	cane
yīng táo	樱桃	cherry
yē zi	椰子	coconut
pú tao	葡萄	grape
hā mì guā	哈密瓜	hami melon
zǎo	枣	jujube
mí hóu táo	猕猴桃	kiwi fruit / Chinese gooseberry
jīn jú	金橘	kumquat
lì zhī	荔枝	litchi fruit
máng guǒ	芒果	mango
xiāng guā	香瓜	muskmelon
mù guā	木瓜	papaya

táo zi	桃子	peach
lí	梨	pear
shì zi	柿子	persimmon
bō luó	菠萝	pineapple
lǐ zǐ	李子	plum
yòu zi	柚子	pomelo / shaddock
cǎo méi	草莓	strawberry
shí liú	石榴	pomegranate
xī guā	西瓜	watermelon

Vegetables:

bō cài	菠菜	spinach
cōng	葱	scallion / green onion
fān qié	蕃茄	tomato
gān lán	甘蓝	cauliflower, kale, brussels sprouts
hóng luó bó	红萝卜	carrot
hóng shǔ	红薯	sweet potato
huáng guā	黄瓜	cucumber
jiāng	姜	ginger
jiè cài	芥菜	mustard plant, leaf mustard
juǎn xīn cài	卷心菜	cabbage
kǔ guā	苦瓜	bitter gourd
là jiāo	辣椒	hot pepper/chili
lú sǔn	芦笋	asparagus
mǎ líng shǔ	马铃薯	potato
nán guā	南瓜	pumpkin
qié zi	茄子	eggplant
qín cài	芹菜	celery

qīng dòu	青豆	green beans in gen
qīng jiāo	青椒	green pepper
shān yao	山药	yam
shēng cài	生菜	lettuce
tián cài	甜菜	beet
wān dòu	豌豆	pea
wō jù	莴苣	lettuce
wú jīng	芜菁	turnip
xī hóng shì	西红柿	tomato
xiāng cài	香菜	parsley
yáng cōng	洋葱	onion
yáng yù	洋芋	potato
yù mǐ	玉米	corn / maize

Clothes:

mào yì	贸易	(commercial) trade
xī zhuāng	西装	(Western-style) clothes
pī fēng	披风	ancient lady's cloak
qiú xié	球鞋	athletic shoes
xuē	靴	boots, leg and neck of the boot
xuē zi	靴子	boots; Wellingtons
qí páo	旗袍	Chinese-style dress / cheongsam
biàn xié	便鞋	cloth shoes / slippers
guà	褂	coat
wài tào	外套	coat
shǒu tào	手套	glove / mitten
cháng páo	长袍	gown
mào zi	帽子	hat / cap
kuī	盔	helmet
hé fú	和服	Japanese dress
pí xié	皮鞋	leather shoes
chāo duǎn qún	超短裙	miniskirt

shuì yī	睡衣	pajamas
chèn kù	衬裤	panties
chèn qún	衬裙	petticoat
yǔ xié	雨鞋	rain boots
liáng xié	凉鞋	sandal
wéi jīn	围巾	scarf / shawl
chèn shān	衬衫	shirt / blouse
chèn shān	衬衫	shirt / blouse
xié	鞋	shoe
xié dǐ	鞋底	shoe sole
xié dài	鞋带	shoelace, shoestring
xié yóu	鞋油	shoeshine, shoe cream
bīng xié	冰鞋	skating boots / skates
qún zi	裙子	skirt
tuō xié	拖鞋	slippers
duǎn wà	短袜	sock
wà zi	袜子	socks / stockings
pí dài	皮带	strap / leather belt
cǎo xié	草鞋	straw sandal

yàn wěi fú	燕尾服	swallow-tailed (coat)
xié gēn	鞋跟	the heel of a shoe
kù zi	裤子	trousers / pants
nèi kù	内裤	underwear
zhì fù	制服	uniform
lā liàn	拉链	zipper

Parts of the Body:

jiǎo huái	脚踝	ankle
gē bo	胳膊	arm
shǒu bì	手臂	arm
tún	臀	butt / buttocks
xiōng	胸	chest/bosom/mind/heart/thorax
zhǒu	肘	elbow / pork shoulder
nǔ xìng	女性	female
jiǎo	脚	foot/kick/role
shǒu	手	hand/wrist
tóu	头	head
xī	膝	knee
xī gài	膝盖	knee
tuǐ	腿	leg
nán xìng	男性	male
jǐng	颈	neck
rǔ tóu	乳头	nipple
kuān	髋	pelvis / pelvic

jiān	肩	shoulder
shǒu wàn	手腕	skill / finesse
fù	腹	stomach/ abdomen /belly
rǔ fáng	乳房	the breasts
xiǎo tuǐ	小腿	the calf
dà tuǐ	大腿	thigh
kuà	胯	thigh / leg
dǔ	肚	tripe/belly
yāo	腰	waist
zhì	痣	birthmark / mole
liǎn jiá	脸颊	cheek
xià ba	下巴	chin
yá chǐ	牙齿	dental / tooth
jiǔ wō	酒窝	dimple
ěr duo	耳朵	ear
yǎn jīng	眼睛	eye
méi mao	眉毛	eyebrow
yǎn pí	眼皮	eyelid

qián è	前额	forehead
què bān	雀斑	freckle
tóu fa	头发	hair (on the head)
jié máo	睫毛	lash
chún	唇	lip; lips
ěr chuí	耳垂	lower ear lobe
zuǐ	嘴	mouth
zuǐ bā	嘴巴	mouth
bí zi	鼻子	nose
bí kǒng	鼻孔	nostril
máo kǒng	毛孔	pore
pí fū	皮肤	skin
zhòu wén	皱纹	wrinkle
jiǎo huái	脚踝	ankle
zhī jia	指甲	fingernail
zhǐ wén	指纹	fingerprint
quán tóu	拳头	fist
shí zhǐ	食指	forefinger
zhī guān	指关	knuckle

jié	节	
shǒu zhǎng	手掌	palm
shǒu wàn	手腕	skill / finesse
zhōng zhǐ	中指	the middle finger
jiǎo zhǐ	脚趾	toe
dà cháng	大肠	the large intestine
dòng mài	动脉	artery
fèi	肺	lung
gān zàng	肝脏	liver
héng gé mó	横膈膜	(physiol.) the diaphragm
jiǎ zhuàng xiàn	甲状腺	thyroid gland
jìng mài	静脉	vein
lán wěi	阑尾	appendix (in human body)
páng guāng	膀胱	urine bladder
pí zàng	脾脏	the pancreas
qì guǎn	气管	(physiol.) the windpipe, trachea; the bronchial tubes

shén jīng	神经	nerve
shèn zàng	肾脏	kidney
wèi	胃	stomach
xiàn	腺	gland
xiǎo cháng	小肠	the intestines
xīn zàng	心脏	heart
hóu jié	喉结	Adam's' apple
nǎo	脑	brain
shí guǎn	食管	esophagus
lìn bā xì tǒng	淋巴系统	lymphatic system
yān	咽	narrow pass / throat
shàng è	上颚	roof of mouth
yān hóu	咽喉	the throat
hóu lóng	喉咙	throat
hóu tóu	喉头	throat / larynx
shé	舌	tongue
shēng dài	声带	vocal cord(s)

Parts of the House:

Pinyin	Chinese	English
yùshì	浴室	bathroom
wòshì	卧室	bedroom
fàntīng	饭厅	dining room
chúfáng	厨房	kitchen
kètīng	客厅	living room
zhǔrén fáng wò	主人房卧	master bedroom
xià chén	下沉	sink
kòngyú de fángjiān	空余的房间	spare room
shūfáng yánjiū	书房研究	study
mǎtǒng	马桶	toilet
yuánzi	园子	garden
yángtái	阳台	balcony
zǒuláng yángtái	走廊阳台	veranda
mén	门	door
shìchuāng hù	视窗户	windows
lóu shàng	楼上	upstairs
lóu xià	楼下	downstairs

chuáng	床	bed
tǎnzi	毯子	blanket
yǐ zi	椅子	chairs
chōutì guì	抽屉柜	chest of drawers
chájī	茶几	coffee table
kàodiàn	靠垫	cushions
bàngōng zhuō	办公桌	desk
huāhuì	花卉	flowers
chuáng diàn	床垫	mattress
zhěntou	枕头	pillows
zhíwù	植物	plants
bèizi	被子	quilt
biǎo chuángdān	表床单	sheets
shāfā	沙发	sofa
biǎo	表	table
yīguì	衣柜	wardrobe

Office and Computer Equipment:

Pinyin	Chinese	English
lán guāngdié jī	蓝光碟机	Blue-Ray machine
shèxiàngjī	摄像机	camcorder
guāngpán	光盘	CD
jīguāng chàngjī	激光唱机	CD player
jìsuànjī	计算机	computer
diànnǎo shèbèi	电脑设备	computer equipment
DVD bòfàng jī	DVD 播放机	DVD player
chuánzhēn jī	传真机	fax machine
jiànpán	键盘	keyboard
bǐjìběn diànnǎo	笔记本电脑	laptop
xiǎnshìqì	显示器	monitor
shǔbiāo	鼠标	mouse
dǎyìnjī	打印机	printer
sǎomiáo yí	扫描仪	scanner
ruǎnjiàn	软件	software
diànshì	电视	television

Money and Banking Terms:

Pinyin	Chinese	English
yīngbàng	英镑	British pound
yìngbì	硬币	coins
xìnyòngkǎ	信用卡	credit cards
huòbì	货币	currency
ōuyuán	欧元	Euro
huìlǜ	汇率	exchange rate
cáizhèng	财政	finance
gǎngyuán	港元	Hong Kong dollar
rìyuán	日圆	Japanese yen
zhōngguó dàlù de qián	中国大陆的钱	Mainland Chinese money
qián	钱	money
zhǐbì	纸币	paper money
xīnjiāpō yuan	新加坡元	Singapore dollar
xīn táibì	新台币	Taiwan dollar
měiyuán	美元	US dollar

Occupations:

Pinyin	Chinese	English
kuàijì	会计	accountant
yǎnyuán	演员	actor
yínháng jiā	银行家	banker
yīshēng	医生	doctor
biānjí	编辑	editor
diàngōng	电工	electrician
fēijī fúwùyuán	飞机服务员	flight attendant
lùshī	律师	lawyer
yīnyuè rén	音乐人	musician
hùshì	护士	nurse
bàngōngshì jīnglǐ	办公室经理	office manager
yáchǐ jiàozhèng yīshēng	牙齿校正医生	orthodontist
fēixíngyuán	飞行员	pilot
guǎn gōng	管工	plumber
yóudìyuán	邮递员	postman
jiàoshòu	教授	professor
qiántái	前台	receptionist

mìshū	秘书	secretary
cáiféng	裁缝	tailor
chūzū chē sījī	出租车司机	taxi driver
lǎoshī	老师	teacher
huǒchē sījī	火车司机	train driver
zuòjiā	作家	writer

Animals:

dòngwù	动物	animals
niǎo	鸟	bird
māo	猫	cat
nǎiniú	奶牛	cow
lù	鹿	deer
gǒu	狗	dog
dàxiàng	大象	elephant
chángjǐnglù	长颈鹿	giraffe
shānyáng	山羊	goat
xīngxing	猩猩	gorilla
mǎ	马	horse
hóuzi	猴子	monkey
lǎoshǔ	老鼠	mouse
niú	牛	ox
zhū	猪	pig
mǎjū	马驹	pony

Countries:

Pinyin	Simplified	Traditional	Countries
āfùhàn	阿富汗	阿富汗	Afghanistan
āěrbāníyà	阿尔巴尼亚	阿爾巴尼亞	Albania
měizhōu sàmóyà	美洲萨摩亚	美洲薩摩亞	American Samoa
ā gēn tíng	阿根廷	阿根廷	Argentina
yàměiníyà	亚美尼亚	亞美尼亞	Armenia
yàzhōu	亚洲	亞洲	Asia
àozhōu	澳洲	澳洲	Australia
àodìlì	奥地利	奥地利	Austria
āsàibàijiāng	阿塞拜疆	阿塞拜疆	Azerbaijan
bāhāmǎ	巴哈马	巴哈馬	Bahamas
bālín	巴林	巴林	Bahrain
mèngjiālāguó	孟加拉国	孟加拉國	Bangladesh
bābèiduō	巴贝多	巴貝多	Barbados
báiéluósī	白俄罗斯	白俄羅斯	Belarus
bǐlìshí	比利时	比利時	Belgium
bōlìwéiyà	玻利维亚	玻利維亞	Bolivia

bā xī	巴西	巴西	Brazil
bǎojiālìyà	保加利亚	保加利亞	Bulgaria
jiǎnpǔzhài	柬埔寨	柬埔寨	Cambodia
jiā ná dà	加拿大	加拿大	Canada
zhìlì	智利	智利	Chile
zhōngguó	中国	中國	China
gēlúnbǐyà	哥伦比亚	哥倫比亞	Columbia
gēsīdàlíjiā	哥斯大黎加	哥斯大黎加	Costa Rica
kèluódìyà	克罗地亚	克羅地亞	Croatia
gǔbā	古巴	古巴	Cuba
sàipǔlùsī	塞浦路斯	塞浦路斯	Cyprus
sàipǔlùsī	塞浦路斯	塞浦路斯	Cyprus
dānmài	丹麦	丹麥	Denmark
duō míng níjiā	多明尼加	多明尼加	Dominican Republic
dōng dìwèn	东帝汶	東帝汶	East Timor
è guā duō	厄瓜多	厄瓜多	Ecuador
sàěrwǎduō	萨尔瓦多	薩爾瓦多	El Salvador

142

fěijǐ	斐济	斐濟	Fiji
fēnlán	芬兰	芬蘭	Finland
fǎguó	法国	法國	France
fǎ shǔ bōlìníxīyà	法属波利尼西亚	法屬波利尼西亞	French Polynesia
gélǔjíyà	格鲁吉亚	佐治亞	Georgia
déguó	德国	德國	Germany
xīlà	希腊	希臘	Greece
gé ruì nàdá	格瑞那达	格瑞那達	Grenada
guā dì mǎlā	瓜地马拉	瓜地馬拉	Guatemala
gěyànà	盖亚那	蓋亞那	Guyana
hǎidì	海地	海地	Haiti
hóng dōulāsī	宏都拉斯	宏都拉斯	Honduras
xiōngyálì	匈牙利	匈牙利	Hungary
bīngdǎo	冰岛	冰島	Iceland
yìndù	印度	印度	India
yìndùníxīyà	印度尼西亚	印度尼西亞	Indonesia
yīlǎng	伊朗	伊朗	Iran

yīlākè	伊拉克	伊拉克	Iraq
àiěrlán	爱尔兰	愛爾蘭	Ireland
yǐsèliè	以色列	以色列	Israel
yìdàlì	意大利	意大利	Italy
yámǎijiā	牙买加	牙買加	Jamaica
rìběn	日本	日本	Japan
yuēdàn	约旦	約旦	Jordan
hánguó	韩国	韓國	Korea
kēwēitè	科威特	科威特	Kuwait
lǎowō	老挝	老撾	Laos
líbānèn	黎巴嫩	黎巴嫩	Lebanon
lièzhīdūn shìdēng	列支敦士登	列支敦士登	Liechtenstein
lúsēnbǎo	卢森堡	盧森堡	Luxembourg
mǎláixīyà	马来西亚	馬來西亞	Malaysia
mǎěrdàifū	马尔代夫	馬爾代夫	Maldives
mǎěrtā	马耳他	馬耳他	Malta
mò xī gē	墨西哥	墨西哥	Mexico
mì kèluóxīyà	密克罗西	密克羅西	Micronesia

dǎo	亚岛	亞島	
móěrduōwǎ gònghéguó	摩尔多瓦共和国	摩爾多瓦共和國	Moldova Republic
mónàgē	摩纳哥	摩納哥	Monaco
měnggǔ	蒙古	蒙古	Mongolia
miǎndiàn	缅甸	緬甸	Myanmar
níbóěr	尼泊尔	尼泊爾	Nepal
hélán	荷兰	荷蘭	Netherlands
xīn kǎlǐduōníyà	新卡里多尼亚	新卡裡多尼亞	New Caledonia
xīn xī lán	新西兰	新西蘭	New Zealand
níjiālāguā	尼加拉瓜	尼加拉瓜	Nicaragua
běi cháoxiǎn	北朝鲜	北朝鮮	North Korea
nuówēi	挪威	挪威	Norway
āmàn	阿曼	阿曼	Oman
bājīsītǎn	巴基斯坦	巴基斯坦	Pakistan
bālèsītǎn	巴勒斯坦	巴勒斯坦	Palestine
bānámǎ	巴拿马	巴拿馬	Panama
bā bù yà xīn	巴布亚新	巴布亞新	Papua New Guinea

jǐn èi yà	几内亚	幾內亞	
bālāguī	巴拉圭	巴拉圭	Paraguay
bì lǔ	秘鲁	秘鲁	Peru
fēilǜbīn	菲律宾	菲律賓	Philippines
bōlán	波兰	波蘭	Poland
pútáoyá	葡萄牙	葡萄牙	Portugal
bōduōlígè	波多黎各	波多黎各	Puerto Rico
kǎtǎěr	卡塔尔	卡塔爾	Qatar
luómǎníyà	罗马尼亚	羅馬尼亞	Romania
éguó	俄国	俄國	Russia
éguó	俄国	俄國	Russia
shātè ālābó	沙特阿拉伯	沙特阿拉伯	Saudi Arabia
xīnjiāpō	新加坡	新加坡	Singapore
sīluò wén níyà	斯洛文尼亚	斯洛文尼亞	Slovenia
xībānyá	西班牙	西班牙	Spain
sīlǐlánkǎ	斯里兰卡	斯裡蘭卡	Sri Lanka
ruìdiǎn	瑞典	瑞典	Sweden

ruìshì	瑞士	瑞士	Switzerland
xùlìyà	叙利亚	敘利亞	Syria
táiwān	台湾	台灣	Taiwan
tàiguó	泰国	泰國	Thailand
qiān lǐdá hé duōbāgē	千里达和多巴哥	千里達和多巴哥	Trinidad and Tobago
tǔěrqí	土耳其	土耳其	Turkey
tǔkùmàn	土库曼	土庫曼	Turkmenistan
ālābó lián hé qiú cháng guó	阿拉伯联合酋长国	阿拉伯聯合酋長國	United Arab Emirates
yīng guó	英国	英國	United Kingdom
měi guó	美国	美國	United States
wū lā guī	乌拉圭	烏拉圭	Uruguay
wū zī bié kè sī tǎn	乌兹别克斯坦	烏茲別克斯坦	Uzbekistan
wěinèiruìlā	委内瑞拉	委內瑞拉	Venezuela
yuènán	越南	越南	Vietnam
xī sàmóyà	西萨摩亚	西薩摩亞	Western Samoa
yěmén	也门	也門	Yemen

To form nationalities, just add rén 人　(person) to the country name.

Examples:

měi guó rén -> 美國人 -> American

rìběn rén -> 日本人 -> Japanese

Conclusion

I hope this book was able to help you to learn the fundamentals of the Mandarin Chinese language.

The next step is to take your studies to the next level by conversing with native speakers, going on a trip to a Chinese-speaking country, learning to write Chinese characters, and taking up advanced Mandarin studies.

I wish you the best of luck!

To your success,

Henry Ray